SUPERMAN
End of the Century
Stuart Immonen
STORY, PENCILS & PAINTED ART
José Marzan, Jr. INKS
Bill Oakley LETTERS
Lee Loughridge COLORS
SUPERMAN CREATED BY
Jerry Siegel and Joe Shuster

SUPERMAN: END OF THE CENTURY. February, 2000. Published by DC Comics, 1700 Broadway, New York, NY 10019. Printed on recyclable paper.
Printed in Canada.
DC Comics. A division of Warner Bros.–A Time Warner Entertainment Company 

SOMEWHERE IN THE CARIBBEAN, ON THE EVE OF THE TWENTIETH CENTURY.
CAN'T STAY BROUGHT TO IN THIS WIND FOREVER, CAPTAIN --WE'VE LOST ONE COURSE O' THE FORE-MAST NOW!
WE LIE BY TILL OUR EMPLOYER RETURNS, MR. GRAVES. BUT, DEVIL TAKE HER--
"--WHAT IS SHE DOING ON THAT ROCK?"
NO MORE PROTESTATION, CONTESSA DEL PORTENZA. YOU'VE DONE ALL YOU CAN.
COME THE MORROW, FOR MY EFFORTS TO SUCCEED, YOU MUST BE HALF THE WORLD AWAY.
SIGNOR PRIORA, DID YOU HEAR--?
IT IS ONLY YOUR CONSCIENCE, OR THE WIND'S HOWL, MY LADY. COME, YOU MUST NOT HESITATE.
FARE YOU WELL, CONTESSA. CENSOR THIS PLACE FROM YOUR THOUGHTS.
REMEMBER ONLY THAT YOUR SINISTER SECRET IS BURIED THIS NIGHT, SO THAT THE WORLD MIGHT LIVE!
"NEVER RETURN, AND NEVER LOOK BACK."

MY THANKS, CAPTAIN. WE SAIL FOR THE CONTINENT IMMEDIATELY.
THE--? THERE'S A STORM ABOUT, LADY!
WE'LL FIND PORT IN ST. AGETHE, NOT A LEAGUE WESTWARD!
OUR ARRANGEMENT DOES NOT SHELTER COMPROMISE, CAPTAIN.
NAPLES AWAITS MY RETURN.
IF YOU WISH YOUR DEAR WIFE AND DAUGHTER TO DELIGHT AGAIN IN THE FLOWERS OF SPRING, THEN I SUGGEST WE SAIL.
IMMEDIATELY.
MISTER GRAVES, WEIGH ANCHOR!
ALL HANDS, IL MARTELLO HAULS THE WIND TONIGHT!
In the winter of 1899, I locked up one of my pasts and laid it to rest. It was an all-too-familiar occurrence.
But my blessed, expected relief never came, for unlike those other periods of my life...
...this past was not quite dead.
NO!

ABANDON YOUR POSTS!
ABANDON SHIP!
CAPTAIN, WE'VE TAKEN ON WATER!
AYE, AND I'M CURSED FOR IT. THE DAY MY SHIP LEFT DOCK WITH YOU WAS A BLACK ONE, CONTESSA!

No mortal would survive the wreck of Il Martello.

And yet, my thoughts were consumed; Should one day my shameful history be exposed, all would be lost.

AAH!
Not just for me--

--but for the entire earth.

ONE HUNDRED YEARS LATER, THE TURN OF ANOTHER CENTURY.
IL MARTELLO'S LOG BOOK WOULD BE IN A SAFE-BOX THERE, IF IT STILL EXISTS.
I DON'T THINK SO, JULIA. THE CAPTAIN'S DAY CABIN'S STILL ABOUT FIFTY YARDS TO YOUR LEFT.
HOLD IT. YOU'RE RIGHT ABOVE THE QUARTERDECK NOW.
THAT'S IT, ALL RIGHT. COME ON UP AND WE'LL ASSEMBLE THE TEAM FOR A FULL-SCALE DIVE THIS AFTERNOON.
TOO BAD WE DIDN'T FIND IT SOONER, THOUGH. A THOROUGH DOCUMENTATION WOULD REQUIRE ANOTHER WEEK, AT LEAST.
ST. AGETHE WON'T EXTEND OUR STAY, MARK. WE'VE GOT TO BE STATESIDE DAY AFTER TOMORROW.
Ah, BUT I'M BETTING OUR PATRON CAN PULL A FEW STRINGS.
IF ANYONE CAN BEND THE RULES OF GOVERNMENT, IT'S LEX LUTHOR.

WELL, MARK EASTMAN. I TRUST YOU HAVE NEWS TO BRIGHTEN UP A DREARY WINTER DAY?
THE RECOVERY BEARS FRUIT AT LAST, eh? NEED MORE TIME?
I SUPPOSE I'LL HAVE TO REMIND THE ST. AGETHIANS OF THE ECONOMIC ADVANTAGE OF OUR OPERATION. WE'RE GOING TO PUT THEM ON THE MAP.
AND WHEN OTHER AVENUES OF FINANCE ARE OPENED IN THE FUTURE, I'M SURE THEY'LL REMEMBER US. REST ASSURED --ah, IT'S MY OFFICE ON THE LINE-- GOODBYE, EASTMAN...
MR. LUTHOR, I TRIED YOU AT CITY HALL--
I JUST LEFT, MS. WRIGHT. THE MAYOR'S CENTURY PARTY CONFERENCE RAN OVERTIME. IS THERE SOMETHING I DON'T KNOW ON YOUR MIND?
Um, THERE'S BEEN A FIRE, SIR. AT THE BAILEY BUILDING'S DAYCARE CENTER. WE DON'T KNOW, um -- YOUR DAUGHTER--
I WANT MY HELICOPTER AND A POLICE ESCORT READY! I WANT EVERY FIRE TRUCK AND AMBULANCE THERE NOW, DO YOU UNDERSTAND? PULL THEM IN FROM BAKERLINE IF YOU HAVE TO!
THEY'RE ALREADY THERE, SIR--

"EVERYONE'S THERE."
SUPERMAN!
MIZ CEREZO'S NOT MOVING! I-IS SHE--?

RIGHT. NOW--
KRUMP
WE GONNA GET OUT?
ANOTHER WAY...
I'M TELLING YOU, MS. LANE, THERE'S NO WAY I'M LETTING YOU IN.
CAN I QUOTE YOU ON THAT, CHIEF?
YOU KNOW, THE DAILY PLANET WILL WANT TO ATTRIBUTE ACCURATELY RESTRICTIONS PLACED ON ITS REPORTERS.
FOR THE LAST TIME, AUTHORIZED PERSONNEL ONLY--
PAWHUUM
AUTHORIZED PERSONNEL, huh?

THAT'S EVERYBODY. MY X-RAY VISION SHOWS THE BUILDING'S CLEAR.
THANKS, SUPERMAN. WE HAVE THE BLAZE UNDER CONTROL, NOW. THE FIRE MARSHAL WILL MOVE IN FOR INVESTIGATION SHORTLY.
POLI
METROPOLIS
SO, SUPERMAN. ANOTHER HEROIC RESCUE? WHAT'S YOUR TAKE ON THE SITUATION?
WELL, LOIS, IT'S A LITTLE EARLY TO TELL. THE CAUSE HAS YET TO BE DETERMINED...
I'D BE HAPPY TO GIVE YOU THE FULL STORY LATER --
FIRE DEPARTMENT
FIRE
--SAY, OVER DINNER?
WHY, SUPERMAN, I'M A MARRIED WOMAN. WHAT WOULD MY HUSBAND SAY?
TAKE A LOOK AT YOUR NOTEPAD.
MY NOTEPAD...?
CLARK! SOMEONE MIGHT SEE!
YOU DIDN'T. AND IT WAS IN YOUR HAND THE WHOLE TIME.
WHERE IS SHE?
L.
DINNER AT HOME?
CHANGE FOOD
TO LOVE
IN FOUR STEPS
BY EIGHT P.M.
C.

I CAN'T HELP YOU, MR. LUTHOR. YOU'LL JUST HAVE TO WAIT UNTIL IT'S ALL SORTED OUT.
I WANT MY DAUGHTER. AND I'LL HAVE HER. NOW, LET ME PASS.
MY JOB IS TO KEEP THE PUBLIC SAFE, AND I CAN'T DO IT IF I LET YOU WANDER AROUND INTER-FERING.
I'LL SEE TO IT THERE WON'T BE A JOB IN THE STATE FOR YOU TO DO IF I DON'T FIND MY CHILD THIS INSTANT!
GIVE IT A REST, LUTHOR. I'VE GOT HER. LENA'S FINE.
IN FACT, I WAS JUST GIVING MS. LANE A LECTURE ON SUPER-SPEED...
IN FUTURE, LEAVE THE LECTURING TO THOSE UNBUR-DENED BY EXCESSIVE BRAWN, SUPERMAN, AND CONFINE YOUR-SELF--
LUTHOR--?
I WAS JUST THANKING YOU, SUPERMAN. GOOD DAY.

THAT WAS... ODD.
LEX'S PATERNAL INSTINCTS HAVE BEEN IN OVERDRIVE SINCE LENA'S MOTHER DIED IN THAT HOSPITAL FIRE.
TO GO THROUGH THAT A SECOND TIME MIGHT BE TOO MUCH FOR EVEN LUTHOR'S BLACK HEART.
AND SPEAKING OF SECONDS, I'M DUE AT A DAILY PLANET ASSIGNMENT MEETING WITH A CERTAIN CLARK KENT IN ABOUT SIXTY OF THEM...
TIME ME.
DAILY PLANET

--SETTLE DOWN, PEOPLE. LET'S JUST GET THROUGH THIS.
IN FOUR DAYS, LEX LUTHOR HOSTS A GALA THAT WILL NOT ONLY RING IN THE NEW YEAR, BUT A NEW CENTURY. NOW, KENT--
WHERE THE DEVIL ARE KENT AND LANE?
WHOOSH
PRESENT AND ACCOUNTED FOR, PERRY.
DID WE MISS ANYTHING?
...
NEVER SHOULD HAVE LET YOU TWO MARRY.
ahem THIS AFFAIR'S GOING TO BE A MAGNET FOR CELEBRITIES AND DIGNITARIES. IT'S A CHANCE FOR METROPOLIS TO SHINE.
THINK YOU CAN HANDLE IT, TROUPE?
YOU BET, PERRY!
JUST WEAR A TIE FOR ANY INTERVIEWS, SON.
EXCUSE ME, PERRY, BUT I DOUBT LUTHOR'S IN ANY SHAPE TO PLAY BON VIVANT.
HIS DAUGHTER NEARLY DIED IN A FIRE IN ONE OF HIS OWN BUILDINGS.
EAR TO THE GROUND, eh, KENT? FASTER THAN THE PROVERBIAL SPEEDING BULLET. WELL, LISTEN TO THIS...

ACCORDING TO THE WIRE, THAT FIRE MIGHT HAVE BEEN SET DELIBERATELY.
THE MAYOR'S PUSHING THE FIRE MARSHAL TO CLEAR THE INVESTIGATION BEFORE THE CENTURY PARTY.
THERE'S A LUMP SWEPT UNDER THIS CARPET, CLARK. FIND OUT IF IT STINKS OF SCANDAL.
I'LL TAKE THAT ASSIGNMENT, PERRY. I CAN GET LEX--
YOU I HAVE OTHER PLANS FOR, LOIS. REMEMBER ST. AGETHE?
SURE. LAST SUMMER I COVERED THE ISLAND'S FIRST DEMOCRATIC ELECTION IN FIFTY YEARS.
SINCE THEN, THE ECONOMY'S OPENED UP, AND U.S. INTERESTS HAVE MOVED IN.
RIGHT. ONE OF THOSE INTERESTS IS SCIENTIFIC.
ST. AGETHE'S YEARS OF ISOLATION HAVE MADE IT A GOLD MINE OF ARCHAEOLOGICAL MATERIAL.
WHAT? I'M SUPPOSED TO DIG AROUND IN THE TROPICS WHILE SOMEONE PUTS A TORCH TO THE EVENT OF THE CENTURY?
IN A WORD, YES. EXCEPT YOU'LL BE DIVING, NOT DIGGING.
MEANWHILE, AT LEAST ONE OF MY MARRIED STAFF MEMBERS WILL ARRIVE AT MEETINGS ON TIME.
CLARK? IF LEX LUTHOR'S BEING TARGETED WITH ARSON, I WANT TO KNOW WHY. IF SOMEONE'S GOT DIRT ON HIM, I WANT TO KNOW WHO AND HOW MUCH.
BELIEVE ME, PERRY--
--SO DO I.

HUSH, LENA. I PROMISE YOU'RE SAFE NOW. SAFE FROM--
HELLO, LEX. I'VE BEEN TERRIBLY BORED, WAITING FOR YOU. THERE'S NOTHING TO READ.
ERICA. YOU'RE LOOKING WELL.
FOR A DEAD WOMAN.
YOUR EFFORTS TO BURY ME WERE PREMATURE, LEX. YOUR SILVER TONGUE SHOULD TRIP LIGHTLY.
WHAT DO YOU WANT, CONTESSA?
SO FORMAL. DID YOU THINK I'D ALLOW YOU TO RAISE MY DAUGHTER ALONE? I KNOW THE LOT OF A SINGLE PARENT TO BE A THANKLESS ONE.
I DON'T KNOW HOW YOU ESCAPED THE HOSPITAL...

I FOUND YOUR DOCTORS' CARE... LACKING. BUT YOU'LL FIND YOURSELF EASILY RID OF ME...
...YOU HAVE SOMETHING OF MINE.
A WORD OF ADVICE, THEN, ERICA. YOU SHOULDN'T BE SO CARELESS WITH YOUR BELONGINGS.
YOU MISUNDERSTAND, LEX. I MEAN TO CORRECT A MIS-TAKE I MADE ONCE.
I WANT LENA.
TINK
NEVER. SHE'S MINE. YOU MAY LIVE, BUT AS FAR AS THE WORLD'S CONCERNED, YOU DON'T EXIST.
YES. YOU SAW TO THAT.
BUT HERE'S WHERE IT BITES YOU BACK--SOMEONE WILL TAKE THE FALL FOR TODAY'S ARSON ATTEMPT.
HOW MANY OF LEX LUTHOR'S HOLDINGS WILL GO UP IN FLAMES BEFORE YOU'RE ARRESTED FOR INSUR-ANCE FRAUD?
I SHOULD KILL YOU NOW.
THE FEELING IS MUTUAL. BUT WE BOTH KNOW BETTER. IT'S NOT PART OF THE GAME.
AND NEITHER OF US WORKS ALONE.

DON'T MAKE ME DO THIS, LEX. WE'RE STILL MARRIED.
WHEN YOU HID FROM THE LAW, I RAN YOUR BUSINESSES. WHEN SUPERMAN THREATENED YOU, I WAS YOUR SAVIOR.
AND WHEN I WANTED AN HEIR...? AFTER ALL THIS TIME, I KNOW NEXT TO NOTHING OF YOUR PAST!
YOUR PAST IS CATCHING UP TO YOU, LEX. YOU'VE LEFT TOO MANY LOOSE ENDS. LET ME TIE THEM UP.
LET LENA COME WITH ME, AND WE'LL DISAPPEAR. YOU'LL NEVER HEAR FROM EITHER OF US AGAIN.
WHY WOULD I RELINQUISH ALL I HOLD DEAR?
YOU HAVE SO MUCH YOU DON'T RECOGNIZE ITS VALUE. LENA IS A DEL PORTENZA. SHE NEEDS HER MOTHER.
YOU DON'T WANT TO BE RESPONSIBLE FOR WHAT'S GOING TO HAPPEN.
YOU'RE BECOMING QUITE TRYING, ERICA. YOU'VE OVER-STAYED YOUR WELCOME.

I'LL SEE MYSELF OUT, THEN.
YOU'RE NOT THINKING, LEX. ANY ATTEMPT TO EXPOSE ME WILL ONLY CAST HARSH LIGHT ON YOUR OWN UGLY SHADOWS.
IF I LOSE, ALL THE EVENTS FROM OUR HASTY MARRIAGE ON WILL COME UNDER PAINFUL AND PUBLIC SCRUTINY.
IS THAT HOW YOU WANT TO RAISE THIS CHILD?
AND IF I WIN...
...YOUR EMPIRE WILL CRUMBLE ONE EMBER AT A TIME. IT'S YOUR CHOICE.
GRNNNN
GRNNNN
CHUNN
THAT'S A SHAME. IT'S GOING TO BE UNSEASONABLY WARM IN METROPOLIS THIS NEW YEAR'S.
MS. WRIGHT, CANCEL MY PERSONAL APPOINTMENTS, AND SEE THAT MY JET IS ON THE TARMAC IN TWENTY MINUTES. LENA AND I ARE GOING ON A TRIP.
AND GET ME THE HEAD OF SECURITY. WE HAVE A SITUATION.

"I DON'T CARE HOW NICE THE WEATHER WILL BE, CLARK. I'M GOING TO MISS EVERYTHING!"
ANYONE EVER TELL YOU YOU'VE GOT AN OVERINFLATED SENSE OF DUTY?
LET'S SEE... SUPER-HEARING, X-RAY VISION... NOPE, NO SUPER-SENSE OF DUTY.
HA! NO SUPER-SENSE OF HUMOR, EITHER!
B9
I'M GOING TO MISS THAT FARM-BOY EARNESTNESS.
BLAME MA AND PA. WITHOUT THEIR GUIDANCE, MY POWERS MIGHT HAVE MADE ME FOOTBALL'S FINEST WIDE RECEIVER--
"LOOK, LOIS. WE WOULDN'T SEE MUCH OF EACH OTHER ANYWAY. IF THERE'S A MAD ARSONIST ON THE LOOSE, SUPERMAN'S GOING TO HAVE HIS HANDS FULL."
--OR A SAVAGE MONSTER.
LIKE LEX LUTHOR?
I'M JUST SAYING I'M AS MUCH WHO I AM BY VIRTUE OF MY UPBRINGING AS BY THE FACT THAT I CAN--
--HEAR TROUBLE ACROSS TOWN. WE'D BETTER SAY GOODBYE NOW, LOIS.
CLARK? IS IT--?
IT'S A JOB FOR ME.
EMERGEN
EXIT

BUH-PLAM!
WE'VE GONE TO THIRD ALARM AND THERE'S STILL NO WAY!
IT'S GETTING HOTTER--!
AIEEHH!
RELAX, FRIEND. I'VE GOT YOU.
TH-THANKS, SUPERMAN.
ANYTIME.
I APPRECIATE THE ASSIST, SUPERMAN, BUT OUR PROBLEMS JUST GOT WORSE!
WE THOUGHT THE FACTORY WAS DERELICT--BUT THAT WAS AN INCENDIARY EXPLOSION!

THEN WE'VE GOT TO ACT FAST. MOVE YOUR TRUCKS AND PERSONNEL BACK, CHIEF.
ANYTHING ELSE--?
PRAY--
"--THAT THERE'S STILL TIME TO DRAW THE FLAMES UP--
"--UP--
"--AND AWAY FROM THE BUILDING BELOW."

IT'S SAFE ENOUGH NOW, CHIEF.
SAY AGAIN, SUPERMAN? CAN'T HEAR FOR THE WIND YOU KICKED UP!
ANY IDEA HOW IT STARTED?
NOT MUCH TO GO ON BY WAY OF A CONTEXT. THE FACTORY'S BEEN SHUT DOWN AND SUPPOSEDLY UN-OCCUPIED MAYBE SIX MONTHS.
NEVERTHELESS, MR. LUTHOR'S GOING TO HAVE A LOT OF PAPERWORK IN THE MORNING.
"YOU MEAN, LUTHOR OWNS THIS BUILDING, TOO?"
CONTESSA?
ANDREJ, WHAT--?
--WHAT'S THIS?
A SCRATCH. IT'S NOTHING. I ESCAPED BE-FORE THEY--
NOTHING?
YOU CAME RECOMMENDED AS AN EXPERT, YET IT APPEARS THE GREAT ANDREJ CERT IS AN ARSONIST WHO LEAVES BEHIND EVIDENCE!
P-PERHAPS...
...PERHAPS IT WOULD BE PRUDENT TO LIE LOW... JUST UNTIL SUPERMAN--
HE MEANS NOTHING TO US. LISTEN CAREFULLY-- I WILL NOT YIELD A MILLIMETER--
--UNTIL MY CHILD IS ONCE MORE IN MY POSSESSION.

...PAPILIO BAIRDII OR--OREGONY.
--AND THIS?
OREGONIA. FROM?
COLOMBIA.
NAPLES, ITALY. THE SUMMER OF 1818.
FORGIVE ME, SIGNOR PRIORA. I KNEW THIS DAY WOULD COME, YET... LUCA IS STILL MY SON.
I, TOO, HAVE A SON, MASSIMO, BUT I AM PREPARED TO SACRIFICE FOR THE GREATER GOOD.
YOU HAVE SERVED US WELL THESE MANY YEARS, BUT THIS WILL BE YOUR GREATEST GIFT TO THE REPUBLIC.
YOU WERE WISE TO HIDE HIM FROM THE WORLD, WITHOUT EVEN SERVANTS AT THE VILLA TO BREATHE HIS SECRET.
YET NOTHING ESCAPES OUR WATCHFUL EYE. YOUR SON IS IMMORTAL, MASSIMO. HE HAS AN ABUNDANCE OF LIFE--MORE THAN HE CAN USE--
--BUT ENOUGH TO BENEFIT US ALL.
THE CARBONARI HAVE BROUGHT YOU GOOD FORTUNE, MASSIMO DEL PORTENZA. AS YOU HAVE DRUNK DEEP--
"--WOULD YOU NOT NOW EXTEND YOUR CUP TO YOUR BROTHERS?"
ERICA?

WE HAVE VISITORS.
MASSIMO--?
BOY, I AM PAOLO PRIORA, A FRIEND OF YOUR FATHER.
IT IS HIS WISH THAT YOU ACCOMPANY ME NOW. I TRUST YOU WILL NOT DISAPPOINT HIM.
LUCA!
LUCA, DON'T GO!
SILENCE HER. JOIN US ONE HOUR HENCE.
LUCA!
MASSIMO, DON'T LET THEM TAKE HIM!
HUSH, ERICA! THEY KNOW WHAT LUCA IS.
EVERYTHING WE HAVE, WE OWE TO THE CARBONARI. WE CANNOT OPPOSE THEM.
CANNOT--? YOU THINK I DON'T KNOW WHAT YOUR CARBONARI FRIENDS WANT?
MASSIMO, THEY ARE TAMPERING WITH A LINEAGE OLDER THAN TIME! IF ANYTHING HAPPENS TO LUCA--
PRIORA SWEARS FOR HIS WELFARE.
OH, HUSBAND, THEY SEEK TO TAKE HIS LIFE--
"--ALL OF IT."

Somewhere that night, they impressed upon Luca's mind the esoteric instructions of Pythagoras, and the Forty-seventh proposition of Euclid.

I listened as they unified the celestial and terrestrial elements of power...
...and drew the life from his body.

I watched as Priora grew younger before my eyes...

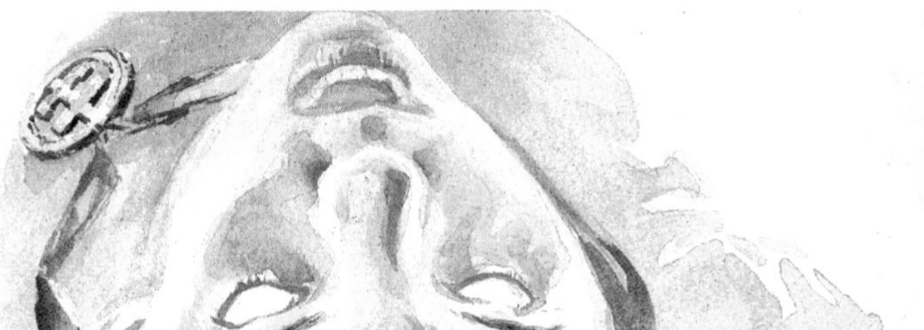
...and knew an old man's anguish as it flooded into my son.

Through the night and well into the next day, it continued. I felt as if in a waking dream--

IT FAILED, ERICA. PRIORA IS DEAD, BUT OUR SON LIVES ON.
I KNOW, HUSBAND.

--a dream that surely would turn into a nightmare.
I KNOW.

IS IT JUST LUCK, MR. EASTMAN? I MEAN, I THOUGHT EVERY LOST WRECK AND SUNKEN TREASURE MUST HAVE BEEN FOUND BY NOW.
NOT HARDLY. READY FOR THE REQUISITE HISTORY LESSON, MS. LANE?
OKAY, ST. AGETHE BECAME A FRENCH COLONY AROUND 1540. FOR THE NEXT FOUR HUNDRED YEARS IT WAS A REGULAR STOP ON THE TRADE ROUTE TO EUROPE.
FULLY-LOADED SHIPS WOULD WAIT IN THE HARBOR TO TRAVEL IN GROUPS FOR SAFETY-- THAT'S THE HARBOR THERE.
OCCASIONALLY, THEY'D WAIT RIGHT INTO HURRICANE SEASON, SINKING BY THE HANDFUL THERE IN THE BAY.
SO WHY HAVEN'T THESE WRECKS BEEN DISCOVERED, OR LOOTED?
ST. AGETHE'S BEEN A MARXIST DICTATORSHIP SINCE WWII, CUT OFF FROM THE REST OF THE WORLD.
ANYBODY WITH THE RIGHT EQUIPMENT HASN'T BEEN ABLE TO GET NEAR UNTIL NOW. MAN, SCUBA WASN'T INVENTED UNTIL 1943!
MUST BE AN AMAZING FEELING FOR AN ARCHAEOLOGIST...
WELL, I AM TEAM LEADER, BUT I'M A FORENSIC BIOLOGIST. A VARIETY OF SKILLS IS REQUIRED FOR THIS TYPE OF RECOVERY.
TRADICCIONES
WHAT HAVE YOU RECOVERED, EXACTLY?
A REAL ODDITY. AN ITALIAN CLIPPER, IL MARTELLO, SUNK ON THE FAR SIDE OF THAT ROCK IN 1899.
THE WEIRD PART IS THAT, ACCORDING TO THE SHIP'S LOG, THEY HAD ONLY TWO PASSENGERS, AND NO CARGO.

YOU CAN READ THE SHIP'S LOG?
UNDER THE RIGHT CONDITIONS, PRESERVATION'S THE LEAST OF OUR CONCERNS-- IN FACT, SOMETIMES ARTIFACTS ARE BETTER LEFT SUNKEN.
SO WHO WERE THE PASSENGERS?

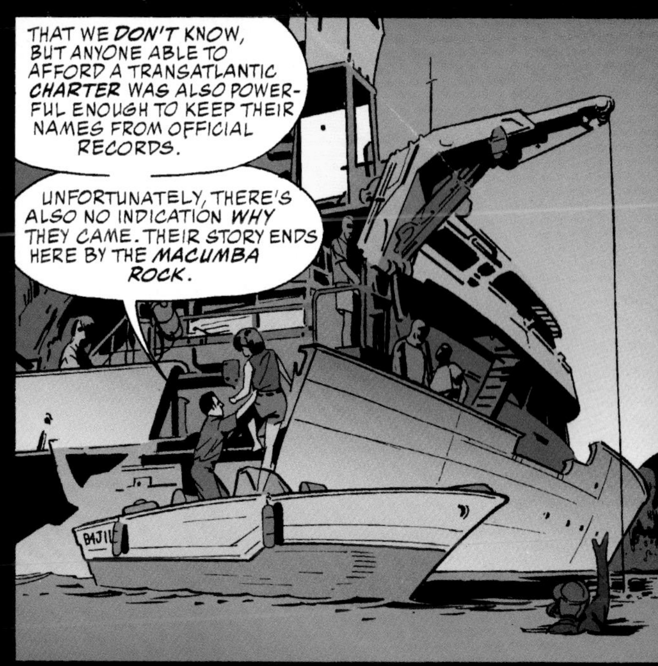
THAT WE DON'T KNOW, BUT ANYONE ABLE TO AFFORD A TRANSATLANTIC CHARTER WAS ALSO POWERFUL ENOUGH TO KEEP THEIR NAMES FROM OFFICIAL RECORDS.
UNFORTUNATELY, THERE'S ALSO NO INDICATION WHY THEY CAME. THEIR STORY ENDS HERE BY THE MACUMBA ROCK.

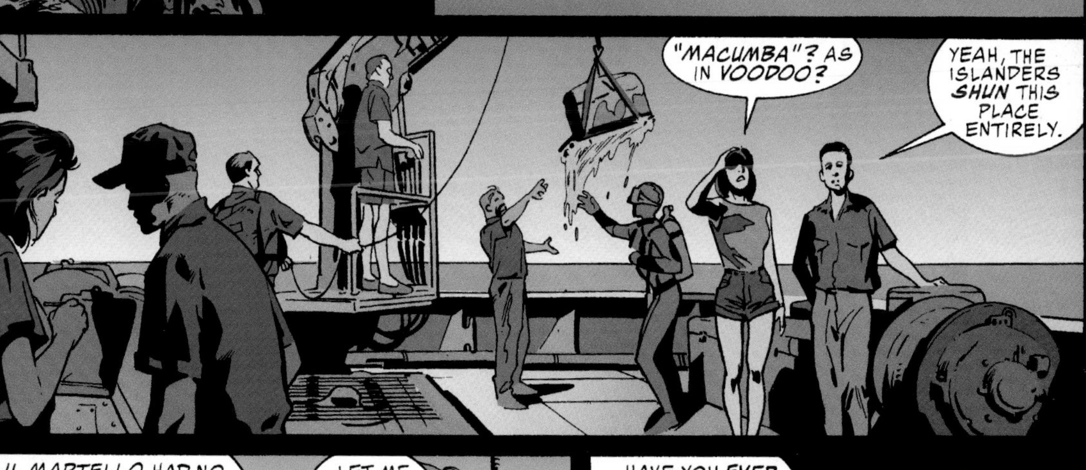
"MACUMBA"? AS IN VOODOO?
YEAH, THE ISLANDERS SHUN THIS PLACE ENTIRELY.

IL MARTELLO HAD NO REASON TO MOOR OUT HERE, BUT IT DID. THE MORE WE FIND OUT ABOUT THIS VOYAGE, THE MORE MYSTERIOUS IT BECOMES.
AND YOU THINK THE MYSTERY'S WORTH SOLVING?
LET ME PUT IT TO YOU THIS WAY, MS. LANE...

...HAVE YOU EVER KNOWN LEX LUTHOR TO MAKE A BAD INVESTMENT?
LEXTR

I'M ALWAYS CAREFUL, SIR.
AFTER ALL, WE DON'T WANT ANY MORE HARM DONE ON MR. LUTHOR'S PROPERTY.
THAT'S THE THING, AIN'T IT?
CHUNK!
NOT THAT I DON'T APPRECIATE YOUR HELP, SUPERMAN, BUT AS FIRE MARSHAL, I GOTTA ASK--
--YOU DIDN'T DISTURB ANY EVIDENCE REMOVIN' THAT WALL--
--DID YOU?
THE BAILEY CENTER WAS A SMOKER, AND THE FACTORY HERE STARTED WITH A LOW-FLASHPOINT EXPLOSION.
ON THE SURFACE, THEY'RE UNRELATED AND ACCIDENTAL--
--STILL, BOTH ON LUTHOR'S DIGS.
I'LL BET HE THOUGHT HE HAD HIS HANDS FULL WITH THE CENTURY PARTY COMIN' UP--!
WASN'T THIS BUILDING VACANT AT THE TIME OF THE FIRE?
YEAH, THAT'S RIGHT.
SOMEONE WAS HERE RECENTLY. AND THEY LEFT A CRIMSON TRAIL.
HOW D'YOU MEAN?
THERE'S FRESH BLOOD HERE. UNTIL WE FIND OUT WHOSE, I THINK LUTHOR WILL HAVE LITTLE INTEREST IN CELEBRATING.

NAPLES, ITALY, 1829.
The silence was thunderous.

By his seventeenth year, I no longer knew the child I named Luca del Portenza.
In his place was a changeling, capable only of replicating the chaos from which he was sired.

The Carbonari removed his restraint, his wisdom, his sense, where they had meant to take his life.
LUCA?

Our once-shared bond now fragmented daily, and I stilled his turmoil less and less.
ERICA, HAVE YOU SEEN LUCA?
I CANNOT BE CERTAIN, MASSIMO. I BELIEVE IT IS HIM--

"--BUT I NO LONGER KNOW HIM."
I HAVE YOU, BASE CREATURE, BUT FEAR NOT--

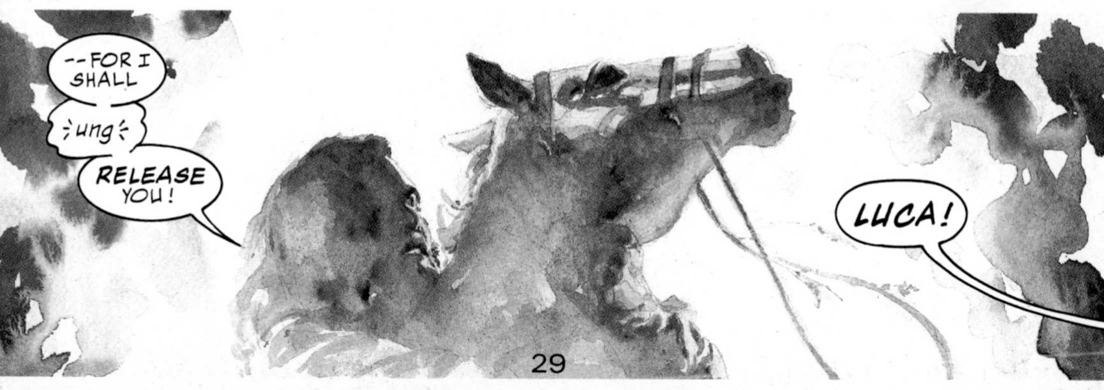
--FOR I SHALL
ung
RELEASE YOU!
LUCA!

CLEAN YOURSELF UP, BOY. OUR PRESENCE IS REQUESTED.
The Carbonari had not died along with Paolo Priora, though their numbers had dwindled.
His own son, Stefano, convinced the remaining elders that their survival depended on recruitment.

MASSIMO! YOU MUSTN'T GO!
WE HAVE NO CHOICE, ERICA. THE REPUBLIC IS DEAD WITHOUT US.
LUCA! DO NOT JOIN THEIR RANKS!
DO NOT PUT ME IN A POSITION TO DISOBEY ONE IF I HEED THE OTHER.
YOU HEARD. THE REPUBLIC IS DEAD...

How wrong they turned out to be.
WE ARE ONLY THE CHILDREN OF OUR MOTHERS AND FATHERS, STEFANO. LET'S ENTER THEIR WORLD TOGETHER, AND WILLINGLY.
I WELCOME YOU INTO THE BROTHERHOOD OF THE CARBONARI, LUCA. THOUGH MY FATHER DIED IN THIS HIDDEN HALL, I FEEL WE ARE TRULY THE HEIRS OF A BLESSED LEGACY.
And so, the initiation began.

ARE YOU A MYSTIC APPRENTICE?
I KNOW THE NORTHERN PART OF THE TEMPLE OF SOLOMON, AND THE FOUR QUARTERS OF THE CIRCLE.
DO YOU DECLARE, THAT, UNBIASED BY THE IMPROPER SOLICITATION OF FRIENDS, AND UNINFLUENCED BY MERCENARY MOTIVE, YOU FREELY AND VOLUNTARILY OFFER YOURSELF A CANDIDATE FOR THE MYSTERIES OF THE REPUBLIC?
I AM PROMPTED BY A DESIRE FOR KNOWLEDGE, AND I WILL CHEERFULLY CONFORM TO ALL THE ANCIENT USAGES--
--AND ESTABLISHED CUSTOMS OF THE ORDER.

I succumbed then to a fever; how long it lasted, I cannot say.
The gift of long life that was our birthright came with a keen awareness of the other's actions and feelings. This gateway through the ether into the mind of my son--

--had become too much to bear.

ENJOYING THE FIRE, MOTHER?

LUCA?

I'VE... BEEN RESTING, CHILD. ARE YOU RETURNED FROM YOUR INITIATION? BUT-- WHERE IS YOUR FATHER? WITH THE CARBONARI?

NO... THERE ARE NO MORE CARBONARI ... NO MORE REPUBLIC...

OH, LUCA...

I DISAPPOINT YOU, MOTHER, WHEN I HAD SOUGHT ONLY TO PLEASE.

I SEE ONLY THAT I STILL HAVE MUCH TO IMPART UPON YOU. WHILE YOU HAVE UNSEATED A SOURCE OF CORRUPT POWER--
--YOU HAVE ALSO UNDERMINED OUR SAFE HAVEN. WE MUST AWAY, AND WITH GREAT HASTE.

OKAY, LUTHOR, WHAT ARE YOU DOING IN ST. AGETHE? AREN'T YOU TIED UP WITH THE FIRE INVESTIGATION IN METROPOLIS?

HMM? OH, THAT. A TRIFLE, I'M SURE. ACTUALLY, IT REMINDED ME THAT I SPEND TOO MUCH TIME AWAY FROM MY DAUGHTER.
IT'S MERELY FORTUITOUS COINCIDENCE THAT MY INTERESTS IN THE CARIBBEAN SHOULD ALLOW US A CHANCE TO CATCH UP AS WELL.
A SHAME YOU WASTED YOURSELF ON KENT...
YEAH, WELL... YOU'RE HERE BECAUSE OF MARK EASTMAN?

HE APPROACHED ME, YES. WITHOUT PRIVATE FUNDING, AND, OF COURSE, INTEREST FROM THE PRESS, THIS KIND OF SCIENTIFIC ENDEAVOR COULDN'T PROCEED AT ALL.

EASTMAN'S PROJECT HAS INDEED PAVED THE WAY FOR ECONOMIC PROGRESS ON THE ISLAND.
AND I SUPPOSE ALL THOSE PINEAPPLES AND SUGAR CANE ARE FOR YOUR SWEET TOOTH.

YOUR ECONOMIC PROGRESS, YOU MEAN.
DON'T THINK ME SO COLD, MS. LANE. I APPRECIATE THE SCIENTIFIC ARTS AS MUCH AS THE NEXT MAN...

I PROVIDE EMPLOYMENT FOR THE ISLAND POPULATION, AND EASTMAN AND HIS GROUP BENEFIT--
MR. LUTHOR! COME SEE! WE OPENED THE STRONG-BOX!
THIS IS IT, MR. LUTHOR, MS. LANE. THE LAST OF THE SALVAGED ARTI-FACTS THAT MIGHT TELL US WHO WAS ON IL MARTELLO'S FINAL VOYAGE.
CAN I TAKE SOME PICTURES?
SURE. YOU KNOW, WE HAD A DEVIL OF A TIME WITH THIS BOX. FOR A WHILE, IT SEEMED SEALED TIGHTER THAN A MISER'S PURSE.
OH--NO OFFENSE, MR. LUTHOR.
CARRY ON, EASTMAN.
SO, WHAT HAPPENED?
NOTHING WE DID. SOMETIMES THESE THINGS ALMOST HAVE A WILL OF THEIR OWN.
I GUESS IT WAS JUST READY TO BE REVEALED.

I'D LOVE TO DOCUMENT IT AT THE LAB IN METROPOLIS, BUT ST. AGETHE WOULD NEVER ALLOW IT.
MAYBE THEN WE COULD ARRANGE SOME STUDIO SHOTS AT THE PLANET.
YOU FRET NEEDLESSLY, EASTMAN. I'LL MAKE THE ARRANGEMENTS MYSELF.
I MEAN, MY PHOTOS MIGHT GET USED TO PROMOTE THE ARTICLE--
--BUT THEY WON'T BE MEMORABLE.
MY APOLOGIES, EASTMAN. I APPEAR TO HAVE RUINED THIS PORTRAIT WITH MY BLOOD.
MS. LANE, I'LL SEE THE FILM GETS COURIERED TONIGHT BEFORE I DESTROY ANYTHING ELSE OF VALUE.
"I HAVE A FEELING THIS DISCOVERY WILL CAUSE A BIT OF A SENSATION BACK HOME."

Constantinople, 1834.
And so, in the years that followed, we traced a route through the Ottoman countries toward India, abandoning the villa and the only life Luca had ever known.
I had hoped, foolishly perhaps, that resuming the burden of his education would be enough to undo the damage wrought by Priora.
I divulged the history of our lineage, and catalogued minutely how unusual our heritage made us--
For a time, he responded, taking easily to a variety of languages, and showing keen interest in culture.
--how, if he took the time to embrace its fragrance, the world would continue to unfold like a rose for him for centuries to come.
--how, as observers, it was our role to remain outside the sphere of human-kind's achievements and folly.
I was naive, and it was an empirical time, and indeed, perhaps I had already forgotten more than he would ever know.
I took his silence for a meditative awe, as if he truly had begun to comprehend all I had told him, never thinking for a moment that he might have ideas of his own.
--SAID, WE'VE LOST THE TRAIL!
The Silk Road, 1840.

THE BEST WE CAN HOPE TO MANAGE IS TO FIND SHELTER ALONG THE ROCK FACE--
I'D CURSE YOU DEARLY FOR LEADING US TO THE TOP OF THE WORLD ALONE, MOTHER--

--IF I DID NOT KNOW YOU FOR A LIAR.

Though I could not understand his tongue, there was no mistaking the Kazak's eyes. He had led us with sure-footed care to his home--

--where he shared with us sustenance and warmth. For a moment, I forgot how far we had come, and why.

I remember saying:
THE ANIMALS --THE CAMELS-- NEED FOOD. I'LL RETURN PRESENTLY.
And I watched him nod knowingly.

And then outside, I tasted metal, and my own blood, and I knew I had made a terrible mistake.

NO! LUCA, NO!
NO...
LUCA, WHY? FOR PITY'S SAKE--
I SHOULD SAY FOR PITY'S SAKE, MOTHER. THEIR EXISTENCE WAS NEAR MEANINGLESS. THEY SERVED THEIR PURPOSE.
THEY HAD FED US, SHELTERED US--
AND FOR THAT KINDNESS, YOU REPAY THEM IN THIS MANNER--?
HEY WERE OF NO ORE USE. THEY RE LESS THAN US, MOTHER.
WE ARE SUPERIOR --AREN'T WE?
LUCA, YOU MUST UNDERSTAND-- WHAT YOU'VE DONE IS WRONG.
RIGHT AND WRONG ARE HUMANITY'S CONSTRUCTS, AND WE--
--WE ARE NOT HUMAN.
WE'LL PRESS ON AFTER THE STORM. THERE'S YET MORE OF YOUR WORLD I WISH TO SEE.

CHF
CHF
CHF
ANDREJ. WHAT HAVE YOU LEARNED?
I THINK... I THINK THE AUTHORITIES FOUND MY BLOOD. I HAVE A RECORD-- IF THEY MATCH IT--
QUIET!
YOU HAVE COMPROMISED US ENOUGH!
I CANNOT AFFORD TO WORK WITH BUNGLERS, AMATEURS... THERE IS TOO MUCH AT STAKE. IF I DIDN'T...
CONTESSA?
SOMEONE'S THROWN AWAY SOMETHING VALUABLE, ANDREJ.
ARRANGE FOR AN OPERATIVE TO VISIT ST. AGETHE. YOU AND I HAVE MUCH TO DO HERE.
Tale of two Centuries:
Luthor's Treasure
by Lois Lane
in the Weekend Magazine
"I'm not guilty" On Death Row
1979 1999
Are we growing?
High Tea with the Queen

"ABSOLUTELY, LOIS. THE PLANET'S ABUZZ OVER THIS FIND. WE CAN'T WAIT FOR THE ARTICLE."

AND THESE PHOTOS SHOW OFF YOUR OFTEN-OVERLOOKED AESTHETIC EYE.

WELL, I MARRIED YOU, DIDN'T I?

HOW COULD I FORGET? I MISS YOU TERRIBLY.

ME, TOO. ANYWAY, YOU'LL HAVE TO WAIT FOR ME AND THE ARTICLE BOTH UNTIL TOMORROW.

I'M BEING HELD PRISONER IN PARADISE WHILE THE ARCHAEOLOGY TEAM PACKS UP SHOP. LUTHOR WANTS TO OVER-WHELM ME WITH MORE EXPLOITS, I GUESS...

WAIT--I KNEW LUTHOR SPONSORED THIS, BUT YOU'RE SAYING HE'S THERE?

HE KIND OF SHOWED UP OUT OF THE BLUE-- WHY?

LISTEN, LOIS, LUTHOR'S IN THE CLEAR CONCERNING THE RECENT FIRES, BUT THAT ONLY MEANS HE MAY BE THE TARGET FOR MORE TROUBLE.
I THINK THE FIRE MARSHAL WAS FAST-TRACKING THE IN-VESTIGATION FOR THE SAKE OF THE CENTURY PARTY, BUT--
CLARK--

LUTHOR'S PUT HIS NAME ALL OVER THIS SHIPWRECK AND NOW WE'VE PUT IT IN THE PAPER. WHEN EASTMAN AND THE ARCHAEOLOGISTS ARRIVE IN METROPOLIS--

--I'LL BE READY.

BEEDLEE BEEDLEE
YES?
YOU HAVE NO IDEA WHAT YOU'VE DONE, LEX.
MY DEAR ERICA. AREN'T YOU TAKING A RISK BY CALLING?
YOU ARE DEALING WITH FORCES YOU DON'T UNDERSTAND.
IF YOU DON'T LEAVE ST. AGETHE NOW, YOU'LL FIND MORE THAN YOU'RE CAPABLE OF HANDLING.
WHAT ARE YOU AFRAID OF, ERICA?
THAT I'VE UNEARTHED A PIECE OF YOUR PAST? COME, WE SHOULDN'T HAVE SECRETS.
LEX--
I'M NOT SHOCKED. I SHOULD THINK IN A WORLD THAT EMBRACED A FLYING ALIEN, IT SHOULD BE ENTIRELY LIKELY I'D MARRY AN IMMORTAL.
LEX, IT'S LENA--
YOUR SIGNAL IS FADING, ERICA. LENA IS MINE, AND SAFE...
LEX--!
WHAT ARE YOU DOING TO MY DAUGHTER?!

NO! NO! I WAS DRAWN TO HER! I SENSED HER--
WHO SENT YOU? MY WIFE?
WHO ARE YOU?
TALK!
I AM STEFANO PRIORA. THE GIRL--SHE IS THE DAUGHTER OF ERICA DEL PORTENZA.
I THOUGHT THE CONTESSA SENT HER--TO TAKE MY PLACE--
THEN IT WAS ERICA!
YES, SIGNOR! WHAT WAS ONCE THE CONTESSA'S IS NOW HERS. I WAS CHARGED WITH THE SAFEKEEPING--
I FOUND THE SHIPWRECK, THE BOX. IT'S ALREADY HERS.
THERE IS MORE, SIGNOR. ALL BELONGING TO THE GIRL.
I WILL TAKE HER TO IT--aak!
I'LL SQUEEZE THE LIFE FROM YOU IF YOU MENTION HER AGAIN.
TAKE ME.

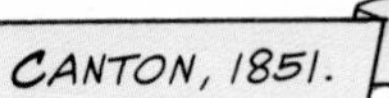
CANTON, 1851.

For ten winters, Luca stained the country-side with innocent blood and abused generosity.
I remained silent, helpless--each ghoulish offense reminding me that Priora had found the immortality he sought, his corrupt soul's desires made manifest in my son's deeds.

Yet all that time, indeed, nearly all Luca's life, I clung to the illusion that he could be turned--
--SHELTER, I SAID. WHERE CAN WE STAY?
MAKE THIS WRETCH UNDERSTAND, MOTHER!

--until he heard the siren song of cannon fire.

The harbor was choked with gunships and the skeletons of their prey.
If ever there was hope in driving out Luca's savagery, it was not to be found under the banner of war.

I THANK YOU FOR YOUR KINDNESS.
NOT HERE, LUCA! NOT NOW!

TROUBLE HERE? Eh?
Years past, I had lost my son's spirit to Priora's tampering and, in the space of a moment, I would lose the rest of him as well.
I MUST SAY, SIR, THIS BEHAVIOR IS BARBARIC.
I DEMAND YOU ACT LIKE THE GENTLEMAN YOU APPEAR TO BE--
--AND FINISH THE JOB PROPERLY.
I THINK HE'S OVERCOME, LADS.
I FELT THE SAME WAY LAYING EYES ON MY FIRST LOVE.
LUCA...

THOUGH THIS FACE IS ENOUGH TO DRAW THE CURTAIN ON A MAN'S PAST.

The very air clarified around the flat click of the flintlock's hammer.
NOW, LISTEN HERE--

--THIS HAS BEEN AN EXCELLENT AMUSEMENT, LAD, BUT THE FUN IS OVER.
I WARRANT YOU'LL FIND YOURSELF FULL OF SHOT MATCH ING SKILLS WITH THOSE BREECHLOADERS.
NOW GIVE IT BACK.

LATER.

HA HA HA! YOUR CONFIDENCE OUTWEIGHS YOUR SENSE, BOY, BUT YOU RECOGNIZE A FINE WEAPON, AND I LIKE THAT.

LUCA--?
UNHAND ME!
Truthfully, I was hardly aware that his flesh struck mine, but I would feel the hornet's sting of his rejection for decades to follow.
Then, perhaps from parental concern, perhaps only from wounded pride, it was my turn to lash out.
HAVE I TAUGHT YOU NOTHING?
YOU BRASH YOUNG IDIOT, DO YOU THINK YOURSELF FIT ENOUGH TO SURVIVE?
YOU'VE NEVER BEEN WITHOUT ME! BY GOD, YOU'LL BE EATEN ALIVE!
Though never had my heart weighed so heavily in my breast--
YOU ARE THROWING AWAY THE WORLD, LUCA DEL PORTENZA! DO YOU HEAR? THE WORLD!
YOU ARE ALONE, NOW AND FOREVER!
--for I knew that forever, like right and wrong, was a human construct, and my son and I--
--we were not human.

HOLD IT! I'LL TAKE IT FROM HERE! WHAT'S YOUR POINT OF ORIGIN?
ST. AGETHE. THE CUSTOMS DOCUMENTS ARE IN ORDER. WE'RE JUST TRANSFERRING CARGO TO OUR HELICOPTER.
MTT METROPOLIS INTERNATIONAL AIRPORT
TAKE A BREAK. UNION SAYS I DO THE LOADING.
WELL... JUST BE CAREFUL, OR YOU'LL BE ANSWERING TO LEX LUTHOR.
HEY, I KNOW WHO I'M DEALING WITH.
YOU EASTMAN? I'M YOUR CHOPPER PILOT. I'LL TAKE YOU TO THE LEXCORP TOWER HELIPAD AS SOON AS WE'RE LOADED UP.
GREAT. WE'RE READY TO GO NOW.
LEX LUTHOR WANTS EVERYTHING UNCRATED AND READY BY THE TIME HE ARRIVES.
"AND IF YOU WORK FOR HIM, YOU KNOW HOW HE HATES TO BE DISAPPOINTED."

TIME FOR A ONCE-OVER BEFORE WE TAKE OFF-- EVERYTHING SECURE?

LOOKS OKAY.
ALL RIGHT, STRAP IN.
IT'S ONLY A FIFTEEN-MINUTE HOP TO LEXCORP.

"WE'LL LEVEL OFF AT 800 FEET AND CRUISE OVER THE DOWNTOWN CORE. A BEAUTIFUL NIGHT TO BE IN THE AIR.

CLIC
"CITY'S GOT MORE GLITTERING LIGHTS THAN A STARRY SKY--"
FWOOSH!
WHAT--?
THE BOX! IT'S ON FIRE!

I'LL GET US DOWN! SOMEBODY GRAB THAT FIRE EXTINGUISHER AND USE IT!

THE CONTROLS ARE LOCKED! WE'RE GOING DOWN, AND FAST!
WHUM WHUM WHUM WHUM

DO WE HAVE A CHANCE?
THUMP!
ALWAYS.

WEEOO WEEOO
EVERYBODY OUT! BEFORE THE FUEL TANK IGNITES!
KRENK!
BUT--THE CARGO--!
COME ON, MARK!
I SAID--
--NEVER MIND.
KA-BRAOOWW!

THE WHOLE YEAR'S WORK --GONE.
NOT QUITE, MR. EASTMAN. THE BULK OF YOUR EFFORTS IN THE CARIBBEAN RE-MAIN INTACT--
--SINCE IT NEVER LEFT THE GROUND.
IT WAS BEING DRIVEN AWAY IN THAT JEEP WHEN I ARRIVED.
HOW--HOW DID YOU--I MEAN, YOU KNOW MY NAME?
I READ THE PAPERS, MR. EASTMAN.
AS FOR HIM, I GOT A RELIABLE TIP. THEN IT WAS ONLY A MATTER OF WAITING.
HE'S ANDREJ CERT, NOTED ARSONIST FOR HIRE. AND ALREADY WANTED FOR CRIMES AGAINST YOUR EMPLOYER.
WHO ARE YOU WORKING FOR? WHAT'S LUTHOR TO YOU?
ALL I KNOW IS THAT FOR MY MISTAKES, I AM A DEAD MAN, AND SO IS LEX LUTHOR.
AND ANYONE ELSE FOOL ENOUGH TO HAVE TOUCHED THAT BOX.

MMMMMGH!

KRASH!
UNGH!

AAAUGH!

LOIS?
LOIS!!

SUPERMAN. AS USUAL, YOUR CONCERN IS APPRECIATED.

BUT MISDIRECTED.
YOU WEREN'T FAR OFF THE MARK, THOUGH. THIS KNIFE MY PRIMATE PAL FELL ON WAS MEANT FOR ME.

COME ON. THERE MIGHT BE MORE WHERE HE CAME FROM. WHERE'S LEX?
HE'S NOT HERE?
Hmm. NO, THE COMPOUND'S DESERTED...
...EXCEPT FOR THE NURSERY.
NO!
DON'T TAKE HER! HE'LL KILL ME!
HOLD ON, MAN OF STEEL...
...WHO WILL KILL YOU?
M-MISTER LUTHOR TOLD ME... DON'T LET ANYTHING HAPPEN TO LENA WHILE HE WAS GONE.
HE SAID HE'D--
I WATCHED HIM GO. HE WAS WITH ANOTHER MAN. THEY WENT BY BOAT--

"--WHERE NO ONE OUGHT TO GO."
ANYTHING?
THERE'S A COLLAPSED CAVE ENTRANCE NEAR THE TOP OF THE ISLAND, LOIS. IT'S ROUGH BUT APPEARS TO BE MANMADE. NO EVIDENCE OF RECENT ENTRY.
MARK EASTMAN TOLD ME THE PLACE IS SHUNNED. NO LOCAL HAS SET FOOT ON THE ROCK FOR A HUNDRED YEARS.
I CAN'T SAY I BLAME THEM. THERE'S SOMETHING VERY WRONG HERE, LOIS. I DON'T SEE LUTHOR OR ANYONE ELSE.
WE COULD HAVE MISSED HIM. MAYBE WE'RE TOO LATE.
KRAKK!
I MEAN, I LITERALLY CAN'T SEE. MY VISION POWERS DON'T PENE-TRATE THE SURFACE MORE THAN A FEW INCHES.
MOST SUPER-STITIONS HAVE A BASIS IN FACT, BUT VERY FEW INVOLVE ACTUAL MAGIC. STILL--
I GUESS WE JUST HAVE TO GO IN.
WHATEVER BROUGHT LUTHOR HERE WAS SEDUCTIVE ENOUGH TO MAKE HIM ABANDON HIS DAUGHTER, HIS PROP-ERTY, AND HIS RIDE HOME. AREN'T YOU CURIOUS?
I'M ADVISING CAUTION.
JUST CROSSING THE THRESHOLD RENDERED MY SUPER-SENSES IN-EFFECTUAL. I FEEL AT NORMAL STRENGTH, BUT I'M VIRTUALLY BLIND--
--LOIS?
AAAIEE!
LOIS!

AAAIIEE!
I'M COMING!
RRIIST
AAOW!
SUPERMAAAN!
WHAT WERE YOU SAYING BEFORE ABOUT MY CONCERN FOR YOU...?

I TAKE IT ALL BACK. WHAT TOOK YOU SO LONG?
NO VISION POWERS, REMEMBER?
I'D START AN AVALANCHE OF ROCK IF I HIT A WALL ON MY WAY TO SAVE YOU.
IF LUTHOR WAS HERE, HE DIDN'T COME THIS WAY.
FUNNY KIND OF ROCK--IT'S REFLECTING LIGHT FROM BELOW...
...AND ISN'T IT GETTING...
...COLDER?
UNBELIEVABLE! IT'S ALL ICE!
IT MUST BE SOME WEIRD NATURAL PHENOMENON.
AND THE CHANGE IN MY POWERS? YOU SAID THE ISLAND WAS CURSED...
YOU'RE BUYING INTO MACUMBA NOW?
MY EXPERIENCE HAS PROVEN SHERLOCK HOLMES RIGHT--ONCE YOU'VE ELIMINATED THE IMPOSSIBLE...
...I KNOW-- "WHATEVER REMAINS, HOWEVER IMPROBABLE, MUST BE THE TRUTH."
YES. SOME THINGS AREN'T EXPLAINABLE BY CONVENTIONAL NOTIONS OF SCIENCE--
--OR RELIGION...

ARE THEY...?
DEAD? I THINK SO.

BUT HOW?
LOOK AT THE POSITIONS. ALL IDENTICAL.
THEY WEREN'T TRAPPED. THEY WERE PUT HERE.

SACRIFICED.
DRAINED OF LIFE.

BUT FOR WHOSE BENEFIT?
TAKE A LOOK--

THIS ISN'T VOODOO.
SLOW DOWN, LOIS. DIDN'T YOU LEARN ANYTHING ON THAT TUMBLE DOWN THE RABBIT HOLE?
DON'T WORRY. THIS ONE DOESN'T HAVE MUCH FIGHT IN HIM.
BUT HE'S NOT AS BAD OFF AS THE OTHERS, EITHER.
MEANING--?
JUST LOOK AT HIS FACE. THE OTHERS WERE JUST HUSKS. THIS ONCE LOOKS LIKE HE JUST CAME FROM A JOG AROUND THE PARK. APART FROM THE MANACLES.
SEEMS LIKE WE'VE FOUND MORE QUESTIONS THAN ANSWERS ON THIS JOURNEY.
I KNOW IT'S CRAZY, BUT I'D SWEAR HE WAS--
--ALIVE, MS. LANE? I'D STAKE MY REPUTATION ON IT.
I'VE NO MORE A RATIONAL EXPLANATION FOR IT THAN YOU, BUT ONCE HE'S AIRLIFTED BACK TO METROPOLIS, PERHAPS WE CAN ASK OUR FRIEND HERE HIMSELF.
LUTHOR! WHERE DID YOU COME FROM?

WELL! IT'S A RARE DAY WHEN I CATCH SUPERMAN BY SURPRISE.

IN FACT, I'VE JUST ARRIVED FROM ST. AGETHE, WHERE, AS OF TWENTY MINUTES AGO, I PURCHASED THIS ENTIRE ISLAND, AND EVERYTHING ON IT AND IN IT.

THE LOCAL GOVERNMENT WAS HAPPY TO BE RID OF THE BURDEN, I THINK.

WHAT DO YOU WANT THIS TIME, LUTHOR?

MARK EASTMAN'S EXPEDITION AWAKENED A SCIENTIFIC CURIOSITY IN ME, SUPERMAN.

MAGIC OR NO, THIS CURIOSITY COULD PROVIDE THE SECRETS TO EXTENDED LIFE, PERHAPS EVEN IMMORTALITY.

ABSURD, I KNOW -- I HADN'T EVEN CONSIDERED THE POSSIBILITY MYSELF UNTIL THIS EVENING.

I DON'T BELIEVE A WORD OF IT, LUTHOR. EVERY TIME I TURN OVER A ROCK, I FIND YOU CRAWLING THERE.

"THEN PERHAPS YOU SHOULD STOP LOOKING, SUPERMAN.
"THIS TREASURE IS GOING TO BE A FITTING SHOWPIECE FOR METROPOLIS'S CENTURY CELEBRATION, AND THERE ISN'T A BLESSED THING YOU CAN DO ABOUT IT.
"ISN'T IT TIME YOU LEARNED, MAN OF STEEL-- LEX LUTHOR ALWAYS GETS WHAT HE WANTS--

"--AT ANY PRICE."

World-weary, I returned to Italy, as I had many times before, to forget. But it was not to be...

I THANK YOU FOR ADMITTING ME, *SIGNORA*. YOU CANNOT KNOW HOW **FAR** I HAVE TRAVELED, HOW **LONG** I HAVE WAITED...

I OFTEN LOSE TRACK OF **TIME**, BUT NEVER A **FACE**, *SIGNOR*. YOU ARE A **STRANGER** TO ME, YET YOU SPEAK WITH AN AIR OF **FAMILIARITY**.

NAPLES. THE VILLA OF THE DEL PORTENZAS. 1899.

YOU HAVE AN AUDIENCE WITH ME BECAUSE YOU SAID YOU HAD NEWS OF MY SON.
NOW... FORTUNE-TELLING IS NOT UNHEARD OF IN CERTAIN CIRCLES, BUT I HAVE NOT SEEN LUCA IN--
--OVER FORTY YEARS, SIGNORA.
CORRECT?

YET YOU LOOK NO OLDER THAN LUCA DID ON THE DAY HE MURDERED HIS FATHER AND SIX OTHER CARBONARI.

I ALONE ESCAPED, BUT NOT... UNSCATHED.
PRIORA...?
THE SAME. AND HERE'S THE PROOF OF IT.

I WAS CARBONARI ONCE, YOU SEE--I HELPED TO UNLEASH SUPERNATURAL FORCES IN YOUR SON, AND NOW--
--IT NEEDS TO BE PUT RIGHT.
LUCA IS UNSTABLE, DANGEROUS, AND BECOMING WORSE. YOU AND HE ARE TWO SIDES OF A POWERFUL COIN. IF I AM TO STOP HIM, I NEED YOUR AID.

THERE IS NOTHING TO BE DONE. HE IS BEYOND MY CONTROL. I HAVE NO--
MY CONSCIENCE WILL NOT ALLOW ME REST--OR NOURISHMENT--WITH THIS EVIL LOOSED, CAN YOURS?
BUT... OF WHAT HELP AM I? I HAVEN'T KNOWN HIS WHEREABOUTS THESE TWO SCORE YEARS!

Ah, BUT HIS EXPLOITS HAVE BEEN NOTORIOUS.
BRITISH NAVY, FRENCH INFANTRY-- HE HAS FOUGHT AGAINST AND ALONGSIDE THE ARMIES OF PRUSSIA, GERMANY, TURKEY, IBERIA...
HE HAS BUT ONE GOAL-- TO VISIT DEATH ON EARTH. WHEREVER HUMANKIND HAS WAGED WAR, THERE HAS HE BEEN.
Fountainhead.
The decoration ceremony
Spectators crowding the Hall fell silent as Brig. General Sir Charles Whelpley approached the platform to decorate the young soldiers for acts of bravery and valour.
I HAVE, ALAS, BEEN ONE STEP BEHIND IN MY PURSUIT, ARRIVING ONLY TO WITNESS THE AFTERMATH.
AND I...?
Lieut. Lucas Deloraine, receiving the Burma Star.
MY FATHER MADE EXTENSIVE NOTES ON YOUR FAMILY --I KNOW OF YOUR MOLLIFYING EFFECT ON LUCA.
WHEN I LEARNED OF YOUR RETURN TO NAPLES, I KNEW HE WAS MINE. HIS WINGS MUST BE CLIPPED IF WE ARE TO ENTRAP HIM.
AS FOR WHERE HE WILL STRIKE NEXT, HE HAS BEEN EXPOSED.
PERHAPS YOU HAVE HEARD OF THE SYNDICALIST MOVEMENT. SOME CALL THEM "TERRORISTS." THEY USE THREATS AND SABOTAGE TO PROMOTE THEIR VIEWS.
Great Republic
SYNDICALISTS MARCH ON CHERBOURG
FRENCH TRADE UNIONS DEMONSTRATE WITHOUT SERIOUS MISHAP
PERHAPS YOU RECOGNIZE A FACE IN THE CROWD.
early waiting broken by su
promptly relieved by po
(Associated Press
ourg, France,
foretold an ugly
LUCA DEL PORTENZA HAS KILLED AND WILL KILL AGAIN.
NO ONE ELSE CAN END IT. THERE IS BUT ONE COURSE...

ARE YOU READY, METROPOLIS?
WE ARE DOWN TO THE LAST HOUR OF THE LAST DAY OF THE TWENTIETH CENTURY!
New Year's Eve
follow the stars to the LexCorp Plaza to celebrate the
End of the Century
sponsored by LEXCORP
RIGHT ON!
THE END IS NEAR!
EXCUSE ME.
WHOO-HOO!
WHERE YOU GOIN', LADY?
FUN'S OVER HERE!
LET'S THANK THE GENTLEMAN RESPONSIBLE, PEOPLE!
LET 'EM HEAR YOU ON LEXCORP'S TOP FLOOR!
CROWDS ARE ESTIMATED AT UPWARDS OF THREE-QUARTERS OF A MILLION IN THE PLAZA ALONE, MR. EASTMAN.
MR. LUTHOR SURE KNOWS HOW TO THROW A PARTY, DOESN'T HE?
NOTHING BY HALF MEASURES, ANYWAY--uh, WHAT DID YOU SAY YOUR NAME WAS?
RON TROUPE, DAILY PLANET. LISTEN, I KNOW THERE'S A PRESS CONFERENCE CONCERNING THE "ICEMAN" FOUND IN ST. AGETHE, BUT I'D LOVE AN INTERVIEW--
EASTMAN, YOUR PUBLIC AWAITS.
SORRY, MR. TROUPE. MAYBE LATER.

FORGIVE THE HISTRIONICS OF EXPOSING THE LABORATORY HERE, BUT POTENTIAL INVESTORS LIKE TO SEE WHERE THEIR DOLLARS GO.
TOMORROW, EASTMAN, YOU BEGIN WORK ON DEFROSTING OUR MYSTERY GUEST, AND WHEN YOU SUCCEED, IT WILL MAKE BOTH OF US VERY, VERY RICH.
MR. LUTHOR, I'VE GOT TO ADMIT MY TRAINING DOESN'T QUALIFY ME--
YOU'RE ON MY PAYROLL --THAT'S QUALIFICATION ENOUGH.
HIRE WHO YOU NEED --MY RESOURCES ARE UNLIMITED-- YOUR CARIBBEAN EXCURSION WILL SEEM LIKE A TOUR OF DUTY BY COMPARISON.
I JUST-- I'M NOT SAYING IT CAN'T BE DONE, BUT IT'S SUCH A LONG SHOT.
WHY ARE YOU SO DETERMINED TO BRING THIS MAN BACK?
HE AND I ARE MORE ALIKE THAN I CAN EXPRESS, EASTMAN. I MIGHT VENTURE TO SAY I EVEN FEEL RELATED.
THERE ARE A LOT OF SECRETS LOCKED UP BEHIND THOSE FROZEN FEATURES. NEW WORLDS TO CONQUER.
JUST THINK WHAT WE'LL ACCOMPLISH.
ANY MINUTE-- ARMAGEDDON.
I DON'T KNOW, LOIS. FOR THE FIRST TIME IN A WHILE, LEX SEEMS HAPPY. MAYBE SOME GOOD WILL COME OF THIS.
CLARK, WE'VE ALL KNOWN LEX LUTHOR A LONG TIME. YOU SHOULD KNOW BY NOW--

"--BAD THINGS HAPPEN WHEN HE'S HAPPY."
LUCA?
IT'S BEEN SO LONG. I WAS FOOLING MYSELF, I SUPPOSE, TO THINK I'D NEVER SEE YOU AGAIN.
YOU'LL FORGIVE ME. I BELIEVED PRIORA KILLED YOU. HE WAS A LIAR AND A MANIPULATOR-- JUST LIKE HIS FATHER.
NOT LIKE YOU. STILL A CHILD-- IN IMMORTAL TERMS--NEVER HAVING LET GO OF CHILDISH EGO.
CLINGING TO LIFE AFTER A CENTURY OF IMPRISONMENT.
I'M GOING TO BRING YOU PEACE, LUCA.
I'M GOING TO BRING US BOTH PEACE.
I DARE SAY YOU'VE IMPRESSED THEM, EASTMAN. YOU'LL BE WELL-REWARDED FOR YOUR RESEARCH EFFORTS--
FIRE!
THERE'S A FIRE IN THE LAB!

FIRE!
STAIRS! USE THE STAIRS!
RON! HELP ME, uh, HELP ME DIRECT TRAFFIC HERE BEFORE THERE'S A PANIC!
SURE, BUT--
RRENNK
TOO SOON...
KNOCK, KNOCK.
ANYBODY HOME?
RRRENNCH!

Hm. LUTHOR'S PARANOIA TOWARDS ME MEANS A LAYER OF LEAD IN EVERY WALL.
AS FAR AS I CAN TELL, IT'S JUST YOU AND ME IN THE ROOM, FRIEND.
AND I KNOW I DIDN'T SET THIS FIRE.
KKKRESH
SPRINKLERS MUST HAVE BEEN TAMPERED WITH.
DON'T GO ANYWHERE, NOW...
FWOOSH
NOT OFTEN I USE HEAT VISION TO EXTINGUISH A FIRE.
THE WHOLE LAB...
SUPERMAN! WHAT HAVE YOU DONE?

I'M SAVING YOUR LAB, LUTHOR--AND YOUR PRIZE.
YOU FOOL. HE'S NEARLY THAWED!
IT WILL ONLY TAKE A SECOND TO SUPER-COOL...
NO--IT MAY BE TOO FAR ALONG. CELLULAR DAMAGE MIGHT OCCUR IF THE CONDITIONS AREN'T--
WHUUUUUUUUUU
DID--DID YOU HEAR THAT?
SUPERMAN, HE'S REVIVED! WE'VE GOT TO GET HIM OUT!
I THINK YOU'RE RIGHT, DR. EASTMAN--
--HE WON'T BE NEEDING THESE--

YEAUURGH!
NNH!
CHINK
KRAKECKK!
NNGH!
UNH!
RRAUH!
SO WEAK ...WHAT'S HAPPENED?
ARRUH!
MY STRENGTH ...GONE...
LUTHOR...
LUTHOR...!
POOR EASTMAN-- JUST AS WELL YOU DON'T SEE THIS...

LIKE FIGHTING MYSELF...
STRENGTH, SPEED--ALL MATCHED...
HNH!
KRUNK
PAOW!
PAOW!
POW! POW!
...
RRRAAUUGH!
NO...

EEAAUH!
YUH! YYAUGHH!
UNNF
KREESH!
WHAT'S HAPPENING?
--FIRE INSIDE!
HERE, LOIS, TAKE MY COAT!
THANKS...
LOIS--?
DID YOU HEAR THAT? IT SOUNDED LIKE--

UP THERE!
CENTURY
IT'S A MAN!
RUN, LOIS! MOVE BACK!
IT'S OKAY, RON. WE'RE GOING TO BE--
VWOOSH
THIS IS THE SECOND TIME I'VE SUFFERED A DRAIN IN MY POWERS BECAUSE OF YOU.
YOU'RE LUCKY I RECOVER QUICKLY.
NOW, YOU SHREDDED INCH-THICK PLEXIGLAS LIKE IT WAS TISSUE. WHO ARE YOU?
WHU... WHO... AM... I...?

I AM DEATH!
I AM POWER!
YOU'VE BEEN BURIED FOR A HUNDRED YEARS!
KRAK
ONE... HUNDRED...?
YOU'RE DELUDED, PAL!
GOODBYE 20TH CENT
00:24:45
GOT YOUR ATTENTION? LET'S TRY THIS AGAIN. THEY CALL ME SUPERMAN.
WHO ARE YOU?

DRP DRP DRP DRIP
TEKK
TURN AROUND. SLOWLY.
YOU WEREN'T LEAVING, WERE YOU, ERICA? I HAVE A FEW ISSUES TO DISCUSS BEFORE THE YEAR IS OUT.
YOU'VE PLAYED THE GAME WELL. IN FACT, I'D EXPECT NO LESS.
IT'S A PLAN OF MAGNIFICENT SCOPE. SOMEHOW, YOU'VE MANIPU-LATED ME INTO UNLEASHING THIS... CREATURE ON MY PROPERTY, MY CITY...
..TO LITERALLY DESTROY ME AND EVERY-THING I OWN.
LEX, NO. IT ISN'T ABOUT YOU AT ALL. I TRIED TO WARN YOU.
WHO IS HE?
I THOUGHT HE WAS DEAD. YEARS AGO. I SWEAR IT.
HE'S MY SON, LEX.
BORN OF MORTAL AND IMMORTAL UNION.

CHERBOURG, FRANCE, 1899.
Memory is selective. I recall with great clarity that it was the coldest August on record.
Priora suggested that wartime had not only given Luca the opportunity to kill, but the grave assura that it was sanctioned.
The hunt gave wa to pursuit, our familial link growi in intensity as we raced through market streets.

HE IS **CLOSE**, NOW. VERY CLOSE.
WE MUST MAKE HASTE THEN, AND **CAUTIOUSLY**. AS YOU SENSE **HIS** PRESENCE, SO MIGHT HE ALSO ANTICIPATE **OURS**.
But Luca's mind was elsewhere.
Four decades of murder in a half-dozen armies only left him with the sharp desire for more of the same.

In every act of destruction, he thought, there lay an act of creation. A conservation of ideology of a sort.
He felt he had yet to create his masterpiece.

But this time, it would not be entirely by his own hand.
This time, he had help.

Agitated, Priora abandoned the carriage, to continue on foot.
HURRY, SIGNORA! WE HAVE SO LITTLE TIME!
BUT HOW WILL WE STOP HIM?

I CARRY THE ANSWER WITH ME.
ONLY TWO OBJECTS FROM THE CARBONARI ARE NEEDED TO SHACKLE HIM.

ONCE TRAPPED, HE CAN NEVER BE RELEASED...
...ELSE HE CONSUME HIS LIBERATOR, AND GROW MORE POWERFUL THAN BEFORE.
THEN WE MUST NEVER ALLOW IT TO HAPPEN.

Brave words.

But ultimately, as our drama played out...

...false ones.

HERE, SIGNORA! WE HAVE HIM!

MOTHER...

THE MANACLES! BIND HIS HANDS!
NO!
USE ALL YOUR STRENGTH!

I--I HAVE HIM...
THIS WILL CONTAIN YOU--
YEARR

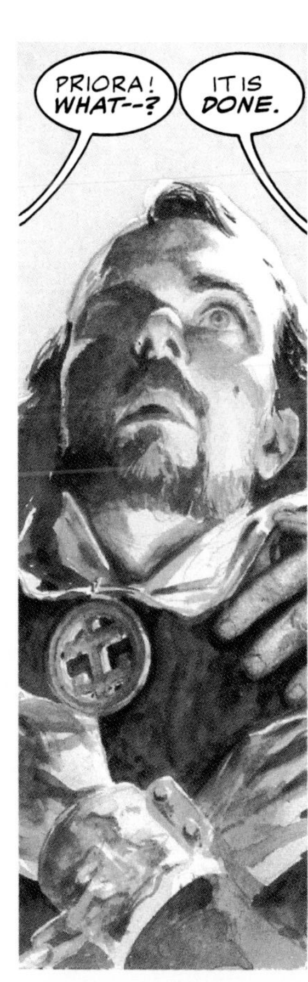
PRIORA! WHAT--?
IT IS DONE.

AND NOW?
I KNOW OF A PLACE, FAR FROM HERE...

"...WHERE WE WILL NEVER KNOW HUMAN INTERFERENCE."

FORGIVE ME IF I'M LESS THAN SYMPATHETIC. YOU LEFT HIM, EXPOSED, WHERE ANYONE MIGHT STUMBLE ACROSS HIM.
I AWOKE A LONG WAY FROM ST. AGETHE, LEX-- PRIORA SWORE LUCA WOULD DIE ON THAT ISLAND. ONLY A CARBO- NARI COULD--
NONSENSE. IF YOU WANT SOMETHING DONE, ERICA--

AUNGH!
KNUNK!

SKSHSHSHS

WHO--?

MY APOLOGIES, CONTESSA...
THERE IS NOT MUCH TIME NOW...
...YOU NEED MY HELP.

YOUR HELP? DO YOU KNOW WHAT YOU HAVE WROUGHT?
YOUR INACTION MAY COST THE WORLD DEARLY. MY SON IS ALIVE, STEFANO PRIORA. WHY? WHY?
THE SAME REASON MY FATHER SOUGHT OUT THE DEL PORTENZAS --TO TASTE THE FRUIT YOU TOOK FOR GRANTED--TO LIVE.
I DID--ONE HUNDRED YEARS SINCE LAST YOU SAW ME--YET FOR ME TO LIVE, SO TOO HAD LUCA.
HIS HUNGER FOR HUMAN LIFE WAS NEVER STILLED--TO KEEP HIM TRANQUIL, HE NEEDED... SACRIFICES.
FORGIVE ME, CONTESSA. I WAS WEAK. WE WERE SAFE, BUT... SO MUCH HAS THE WORLD CHANGED.
SOME THINGS HAVEN'T.
PLEASE. I'VE LEARNED FROM MY MISTAKES. HAVE YOU?
WHAT DO YOU MEAN?
TO BRING DOWN ONE IMMORTAL, THE BLOOD OF ANOTHER MUST BE SPILLED.
YOU HAD ANOTHER CHILD, CONTESSA.
ARE YOU PREPARED TO MAKE A SACRIFICE?

THIS WASN'T THE ANSWER I WAS LOOKING FOR.
YOU CAN'T WIN. WHATEVER YOU DID TO ME, I RECOVER WITH EVERY PASSING SECOND.
THEN YOUR DEATH MUST BE SWIFT, "SUPERMAN"!
YOU SEE, I AM AN ANGEL OF MERCY. I SPEED ALONG THE END OF ALL HUMAN MISERY.
MY DESTINY IS THE ANNIHILATION OF ALL THAT LIVES!
KRAK!
YOU THINK I'LL ROLL OVER AND LET THAT HAPPEN?
PKOK!
YOU'RE A FOOL TO THINK YOU HAVE A CHOICE IN THE MATTER.
I'VE MET YOUR KIND BEFORE--YOU CARRY THE BURDEN OF THE WORLD ON YOUR SHOULDERS, WHEN YOU HAVE THE POWER TO CRUSH IT UNDER YOUR HEEL. I ASK YOU, "SUPERMAN"--
"--WHAT DO YOU SEEK TO PROVE?"
GET THIS CROWD DISPERSED! MOVE, MOVE, MOVE!
ROEBER, HAYWOOD, LOCK AND LOAD! YOU'RE WITH ME!
LOIS, PLEASE...
I SAID BACK, LADY!

WHAT **GALL** TO APPOINT YOURSELF **GUARDIAN** OF HUMANITY!
THEY ARE **LESS** THAN YOU-- **UNDESERVING** OF PROTECTION OR PITY!
MOVE IT, PEOPLE, **PLEASE!** NO ONE SOUTH OF 15TH STREET!
SQUAD CARS AND **BARRICADES** IN A FIFTY-YARD RADIUS!
I'VE SEEN MORE WAR, DONE MORE KILLING THAN A **HUNDRED** MORTALS, AND I HAVE LEARNED **TWO** THINGS--
--**NO** LIFE IS SACRED--
--AND **FINISH** WHAT YOU START.

JUST AS MY FATHER HAD PREDICTED, THE SPELL WILL TRAP AN IMMORTAL-- TRAP YOUR SON-- DRAWING FROM HIM HIS LIFE ENERGY.
THE WAYS OF THE CARBONARI ALLOWED MY SURVIVAL IN THE CAVERN. I PREPARED THE OFFERING CIRCLE, JUST AS MY FATHER HAD DONE--
--ONLY HE STEPPED WITHIN ITS BOUNDARY--
TAKE CARE! STAY WELL BACK!
--AND LUCA DEL PORTENZA CONSUMED HIM.
AND LENA'S ROLE IN ALL THIS--?
FOR A HOMEOPATHIC SPELL, WE DO NOT NEED LUCA HIMSELF IN THE CIRCLE-- ONLY... SOME PART OF HIM.
A HALF-SISTER WILL DO.
THERE MUST BE SOME OTHER WAY...
IF YOU TRULY BELIEVED THAT, WE WOULD NOT HAVE COME THIS FAR.
WE MUST BEGIN NOW, BEFORE A TRAGEDY THAT DWARFS THAT OF THE GREAT REPUBLIC OCCURS.
DO YOU UNDERSTAND THE IMPLICATIONS? NO ONE ELSE CAN RESTORE ORDER.
IF YOU VALUE LIFE, WE MUST BE OF ONE MIND.
TAKE THIS, AND PLACE IT AROUND THE CHILD'S NECK.

uurkk
YOU KNOW, I OUGHT TO THANK YOU. I ALMOST FORGOT THE TACTILE PLEASURE OF IT... WITH MY OWN HANDS...
HAVE YOU EVER TASTED FEAR, SUPERMAN?
S-SURE...
...TASTES LIKE CHICKEN.
K-POW
UNNGH!
SKEEEEE
HONK
HONNK

SKREEEEEEEEEE
HEY!
WATCH--!
OH MY SWEET--!
KWHUMP
KWANG
SKREEEEEEKKUMPFF!

LOOK!
WHAT HAVE I DONE?
tak
tak
tak
CREEEK
GRRNNN
;hff-hff; DONE?
YOU'VE ;hff; GIVEN ME LIFE, SUPERMAN.
NOW ;unh; HOW BEST TO USE IT?

READY TO FIRE ON MY MARK!
WAIT! YOU'LL IGNITE THE FUEL!
HOW--HOW WAS IT YOU LIVED SO LONG, BURIED BENEATH THE GROUND, PRIORA?
I TOLD YOU. I TOLD YOU. MY FATHER'S EXPERIMENTS WITH THE CARBONARI ALLOWED ME TO TAKE HIS LIFE FORCE-- BUT HE WAS TOO STRONG!
I FAILED! LOOK HOW IT LEFT ME! THIS IS NOT LIVING!
THEN WHY DIDN'T YOU JUST DIE?
WHAT DO YOU VALUE MORE, SUPERMAN?
A FEW LIVES NOW, OR THE REST OF THE WORLD LATER?

ALL LIFE IS VALUABLE-- EVEN YOURS.
THINK BACK --I RESCUED YOU WITHOUT HESITATION--
--AND I'D DO IT AGAIN.
RESCUE ME? ;unh; AS IF IT WERE POSSIBLE.
I SUPPOSE YOU OFTEN WASTE YOUR GREAT STRENGTH ON THESE HELPLESS WRETCHES. I'M NOT ONE OF THEM, SUPER-MAN. I'M STRONGER THAN THEM.
IT GIVES ME THE RIGHT TO DO AS I PLEASE.
NO. STRENGTH GIVES ONE RESPONSIBILITY, NOT RIGHTS.
THEN LET THE DEATHS OF ALL HUMANITY REST ON YOUR WORTHY SHOULDERS.
YOU HAVE TAKEN ME FOR A FOOL, PRIORA, AND YOU HAVE NEARLY BEEN RIGHT. YOU HAVE DINED ON MY SON'S IMMORTALITY FOR A CENTURY--
--AND NOW YOU WANT MY DAUGHTER.
CORRECT?
I...
GIVE ME THAT CHILD!
I AM TOO OLD FOR THIS.
YOU NEVER HAD ANY INTENTION OF SAVING ANYONE BUT YOURSELF. YOUR DESIRE FOR EVER-LASTING LIFE HAS SOURED YOUR SOUL.
YOU ARE AS MALIGNANT AS YOUR FATHER, WHO ALSO ONCE PREYED ON AN INNOCENT CHILD--
--MY SON.
;urrk;

IT ;kak; IS BUT ONE MORE CRIME IN A LONG LIST, SIGNORA.
I HAVE LIED, STOLEN, MURDERED TO LIVE THIS LONG, AND ;ukk; FOR WHAT? TO BE A SLAVE TO LUCA DEL PORTENZA'S HUNGER!
THIS CHILD WILL NEVER KNOW THE LIFE SHE MISSED, BUT I--
--I HAVE SAMPLED IMMORTALITY!
WHOOOO
;gasp;
AAAH!
HELP! HELP!
FWOOSH
I HAVE YOU!
NO! NOOO!

WHAT--WHAT IS HAPPENING?
PASSHH
PUNTCH
PTASH
WHAT--?
HEY! WHERE'S--?
WHOOSH
EEEEK!
THAT'S THE LAST OF THEM, SERGEANT!
IT AIN'T OVER, SUPERMAN! LOOK!

IT SEEMS IMMORTALITY IS TASTING YOU, PRIORA.
MAY IT DRINK DEEP.
NOOOO!
NOOOO!
GET EVERYONE BACK.

LOOK OUT!
MOVE!
CAN'T
CLARK...
MOTHER...
...SAVE ME...
...SAVE YOUR LUCA...

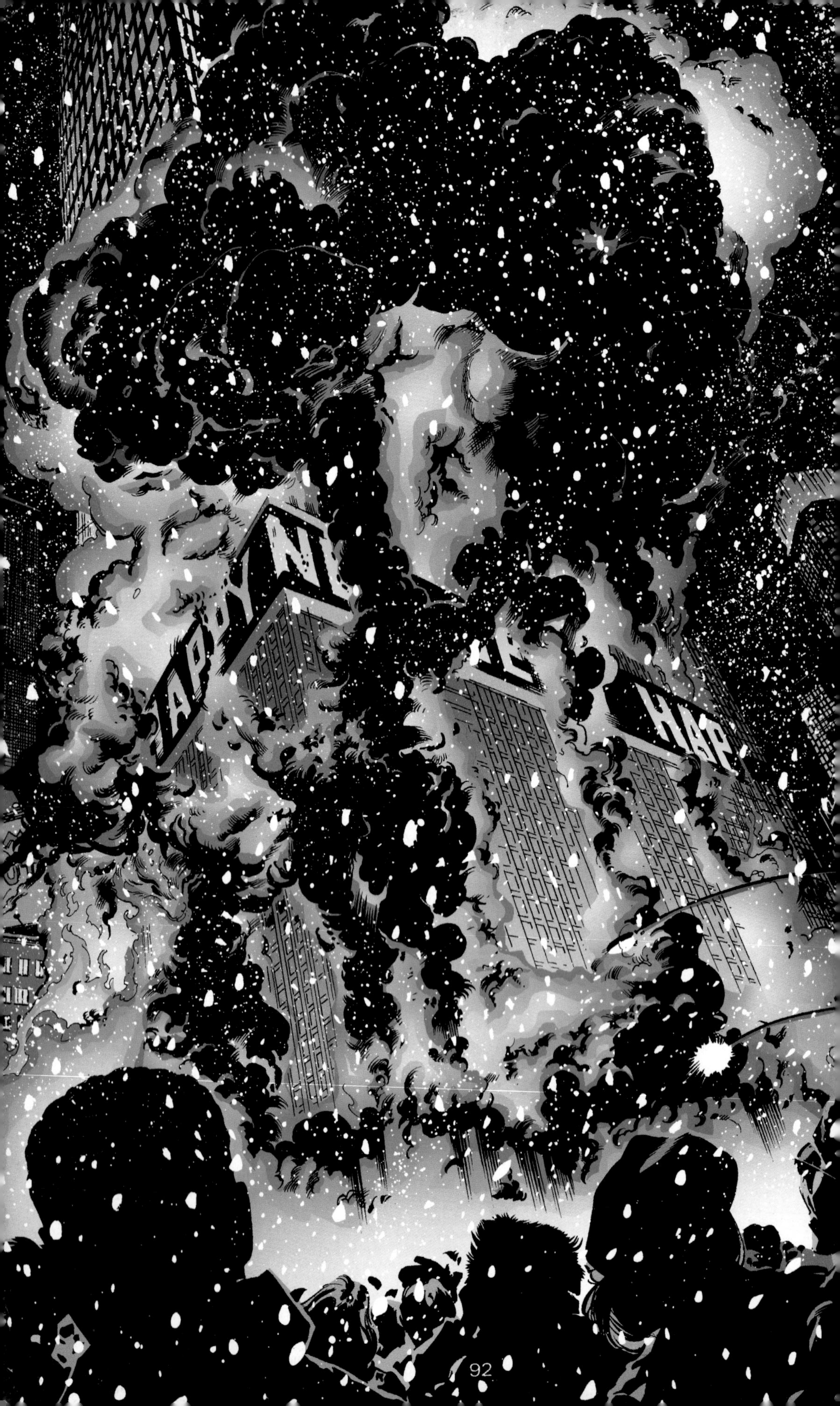

AT LEAST YOU DIDN'T LIE ABOUT THE CIRCLE.

I FAILED YOU, LUCA. ALL YOUR LIFE.
I ABANDONED YOU WHEN YOU NEEDED ME MOST. I... DIDN'T TRY HARD ENOUGH TO PREVENT THIS...
...I MADE A POOR MOTHER, INDEED.

WELL PUT.
LEX?
I SAW IT ALL, ERICA. I SAW YOU DO THE RIGHT THING. I SAW YOU SAVE OUR DAUGHTER.

GIVE HER TO ME NOW. IT'S THE RIGHT THING TO DO. UNLESS YOU'VE FORGOTTEN--
--I HAVE EVERYTHING I NEED TO DESTROY YOU RIGHT HERE.

SUPERMAN! WHAT HAPPENED? ARE YOU-- IS EVERYTHING ALL RIGHT?
I THINK THE CRISIS IS OVER, IF THAT'S WHAT YOU MEAN, MS. LANE.
MY ADVERSARY... DISINTEGRATED IN MY HANDS, AND I'M BACK UP TO FULL STRENGTH.
FOR A MOMENT, I WASN'T SURE IF ANY OF US WOULD MAKE IT--

--BUT YOU ALWAYS MANAGE TO ENSURE THAT IS NOT THE CASE, SUPERMAN.
I WANT TO THANK YOU FOR ALL YOU'VE DONE.
IT'S WHAT I'M HERE FOR, LUTHOR.
YES. SO IT SEEMS. DID HE... SAY ANYTHING? BEFORE HE EXPIRED?
YES, ODDLY. HIS NAME.
Hmm. I SEE. THE DEL PORTENZAS CONTINUE TO HAUNT ME.
DEL PORTENZA? LUTHOR, HE TOLD ME HIS FIRST NAME!
DIDN'T YOU KNOW? THE LOGBOOK FROM THE SHIPWRECK REVEALED HIM TO BE A RELATIVE OF MY LATE WIFE. I'M CERTAIN YOUR FRIEND KENT HEARD...
LUTHOR, SOMETIMES YOU'RE A TERRIBLE LIAR. IF THE CONTESSA'S INVOLVED--!
OH, LEX! LENA'S HURT!
NO.
IT MUST BE SOMEONE ELSE'S BLOOD.
HAPPY NEW YEAR, SUPERMAN.
I NEED TO TAKE ONE LAST SWEEP AROUND, LOIS. THE CONTESSA'S PROVEN TO BE AS CONNIVING AS LUTHOR HIMSELF...
YOU'RE KIDDING. YOU REALLY THINK SHE'S ALIVE?

FOLKTALES SAY: IF SHE'S NOT *DEAD*--

--THEN SHE'S LIVING HAPPILY *STILL*.

Much later...

I had a thought... I'll let Lex think he's won, for one day, not so long from now, perhaps in another hundred years...

...when Lena is a strong young woman...

...she will wonder why her father's world has crumbled and fallen away from her like a chrysalis.

And on that day, I'll be there for her.

In time.